ALL AROUND THE WORLD
AN ILLUSTRATED
ATLAS

Published by Evans Brothers Limited
2A Portman Mansions
Chiltern Street
London W1M 1LE

© copyright Evans Brothers Limited 1996

British Library Cataloguing in Publication Data. A catalogue record for this book is available from the British Library.

First published 1996

Printed in Spain by GRAFO, S.A. – Bilbao

ISBN 0 237 51520 2 (cased)
ISBN 0 237 51631 4 (paperback)

Consultant: Stephen Watts
Editorial: Charlotte Evans
Design: Neil Sayer
Maps: Hardlines
Production: Jenny Mulvanny

The pictures on the cover show:
(**top left**) Boys in typical canoes of the Amazon region
(**top right**) The River Ganges in Varanasi, India
(**bottom left**) Boat cutting through the ice in the Antarctic
(**bottom right**) Ayres Rock, Australia
(**back cover**) Grand Canyon in Arizona, USA

Acknowledgements

For permission to reproduce copyright material, the author and publishers gratefully acknowledge the following:

Cover (top right) Luiz Claudio Marigo/Bruce Coleman Ltd, (top left) G. Hellier/Robert Harding Picture Library, (bottom right) J.Bennett/Zefa, (bottom left) John Lythgoe/Planet Earth Pictures. **Page 4** Arthus Bertrand/Robert Harding Picture Library. **Page 5** Robert Harding Picture Library. **Page 10** (top) Geoff Dore/Bruce Coleman Ltd, (bottom) Paul Harris/Royal Geographical Society. **Page 11** Roy Rainford/Robert Harding Picture Library. **Page 12** Paul Harris/Royal Geographical Society. **Page 14** (left) Norbert Schwirtz/Bruce Coleman Ltd, (right) Martin Dohrn/Bruce Coleman Ltd. **Page 15** Cris Haigh/ Tony Stone Images. **Page 16** (top) Zefa, (centre) Robert Harding Picture Library, (bottom) Paul Harris/Royal Geographical Society. **Page 17** Terje Rakke/ The Image Bank. **Page 18** (top) Luis Castaneda/The Image Bank, (bottom) Drew Geldart/Royal Geographical Society. **Page 19** (top) Adam Woolfitt/Robert Harding Picture Library, (bottom) Robert Harding Picture Library. **Page 20** (middle) Gerald Cubitt/Bruce Coleman Ltd, (bottom) Jen and Des Bartlett/Bruce Coleman Ltd. **Page 21** (top) Robert Harding Picture Library, (middle) Greg Balfour Evans/Greg Evans International Photo Library, (bottom) James Davis Travel Photography. **Page 22** (top) Bruce Coleman Ltd, (middle) Christine Pemberton/The Hutchison Library, (bottom) Gerald Cubitt/Bruce Coleman Ltd. **Page 23** F. Jackson/Robert Harding Picture Library. **Page 24** (left) Robert Harding Picture Library, (right) James H. Carmichael/The Image Bank. **Page 25** (top) Robert Harding Picture Library, (middle left) Hans Christian Heap/Planet Earth Pictures, (middle right) Felix Greene/The Hutchison Library, (bottom) Toby Molenaar/The Image Bank. **Page 26** (top) The Hutchison Library, (bottom) Thomas Buchholz/Bruce Coleman Ltd. **Page 27** Paul Harris/Royal Geographical Society. **Page 28** (top) Tom Learmonth/Panos Pictures, (bottom) James Strachan/Robert Harding Picture Library. **Page 29** (top) Jennifer Fry/Bruce Coleman Ltd, (bottom) Robert Harding Picture Library. **Page 30** (top) Robert Harding Picture Library, (bottom) Michael Macintyre/The Hutchison Library. **Page 31** Robert Harding Picture Library. **Page 32** Zefa. **Page 33** (top) Stephen J Doyle/Bruce Coleman Ltd, (bottom left) Peter Hendrie/The Image Bank, (bottom right) John Shaw/Bruce Coleman Ltd. **Page 34** (top) Robert Harding Picture Library, (middle) Zefa, (bottom) Zefa. **Page 35** Hans Reinhard/Bruce Coleman Ltd. **Page 36** Tony Waltham/Robert Harding Picture Library. **Page 37** (top) Fred Friberg/Robert Harding Picture Library, (middle) Patricio Coycoolea/The Hutchison Library, (bottom) David C Houston/Bruce Coleman Ltd. **Page 38** (top) Steven C Kaufman/Bruce Coleman Ltd, (middle) John Murray/Bruce Coleman Ltd, (bottom) Nicholas De Vore/Bruce Coleman Ltd. **Page 39** Guido Cozzi/Bruce Coleman Ltd. **Page 40** Michael Freeman/Bruce Coleman Ltd. **Page 41** (top left) Luiz Claudio Marigo/Bruce Coleman Ltd, (top right) Rod Williams/Bruce Coleman Ltd, (middle) Brian Henderson/Bruce Coleman Ltd, (bottom) James Davis Travel Photograpy. **Page 42** (top) Zefa, (centre) The Hutchison Library, (bottom) David Lomax/Robert Harding Picture Library. **Page 43** Luiz Claudio Marigo/Bruce Coleman Ltd. **Page 44** (middle) Hans Reinhard/Bruce Coleman Ltd, (bottom) Keith Nels Swenson/Bruce Coleman Ltd. **Page 45** (middle) C Carvalho/Frank Lane Picture Agency, (bottom) Wally Herbert Collection/Robert Harding Picture Library. Back Cover Mr Jules Cowan/Bruce Coleman Ltd.

ALL AROUND THE WORLD
AN ILLUSTRATED
ATLAS

CHARLOTTE EVANS

Contents

	What is a map?	4
	Understanding a map	6
	The World	**8**
	The British Isles	**10**
	Close-up on Northern Britain	12
	Close-up on Southern Britain	13
	Europe	**14**
	Close-up on Northern Europe	16
	Close-up on Southern Europe	18
	Africa	**20**
	Close-up on Africa	22
	Asia	**24**
	Russia and Northern Asia	26
	India and Southern Asia	28
	China and Eastern Asia	30
	Oceania	**32**
	Australia and New Zealand	34
	North America	**36**
	Close-up on North America	38
	South America	**40**
	Close-up on South America	42
	Antarctica	**44**
	Arctic	**45**
	Index	46
	Animals of the World	47

Evans

EVANS BROTHERS LIMITED

What is a map?

A map is a picture of the ground. It is drawn as if you were looking straight down at the ground. A map is drawn very carefully to show exactly where things are.

Different maps show different things. Some maps show the streets and buildings in a town. Other maps show the shape of the land and where countries and cities are. People use maps to find out where things are or what the land is like. A book of maps is called an atlas.

Making map
This is a map of the part of Paris you can see in the photograph above.

Globes

If you could travel out into space you could look down on the Earth. You would be able to see that the Earth is round. You would also be able to see the shape of the land and the sea.

A globe is a model of the Earth as it is from space. Globes are round and show the land and the sea.

When you look at a globe you can only see one side at a time. You have to spin the globe to see what is on the other side. The only way to see the whole world at once is on a map.

The Earth from space

Some of the maps in this book are round like a globe.

Making the Earth flat

The Earth is round but maps are flat. Map-makers flatten out the Earth by dividing its surface into several pieces, a bit like peeling an orange. The pieces are then laid out flat. But between each piece there are gaps. To make a map without gaps, map-makers stretch the pieces so they touch. But this changes the size and shape of the land. Whichever way map-makers try to arrange the pieces there are still gaps. This means that maps cannot show the land exactly as it really is.

Mapping the world
A map of the world is made by dividing the surface of the Earth into segments.

5

Understanding a map

Special words are used to explain maps. Some are explained here. Each map has four basic directions:

North   This is the direction towards the North Pole from anywhere on Earth. The North Pole is at the top of the Earth. It is the most northerly point on Earth.

South   This is the direction towards the South Pole from anywhere on Earth. The South Pole is at the very bottom of the Earth. It is the most southerly point on Earth.

East   This is the direction to the right when you are facing north.

West   This is the direction to the left when you are facing north.

There are four more directions that are half way between north, south, east and west. For example, northwest is halfway between north and west. Southeast is half way between south and east.

On a map, north is usually at the top of the map. Each map in this atlas has an arrow pointing towards the north.

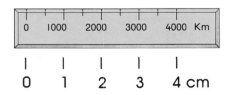

Scale bars
A scale bar like this helps you to work out how far apart places are.

Scales

Because the Earth is so huge, maps show the surface of the Earth much smaller than it really is. A scale shows you how much smaller the map is compared to the real distance on the ground. For example, if a map is drawn using a scale of 1 cm for every 1000 cm of land (which is written 1:1000) it would mean that 1cm on the map would be the same as 1000 cm on the ground.

A scale bar is used to show you what scale the map is. The maps in this atlas have a scale bar like the one on page 6. It tells you that every 1 cm on the map is the same as 1000 km on the ground. You can use the scale bar to find out how far it is from one place to another.

Not all maps in an atlas are drawn to the same scale. This is because some maps show a very small area. Other maps show a very large area. But they all have to fit on to a page. All the maps in this atlas show very large areas.

Keys

Maps also have a key. A key explains the colours and pictures on the map. Different colours are used to show different types of land. Small pictures, called symbols, are used to show the position of things, such as a city or a river. This is what the colours and symbols used in this atlas mean:

Map key
This key shows what the colours and symbols mean on each map.

Key

 Vegetation (the land is partly covered in trees, grass or fields)

 Dry areas (a hot or a cold desert)

 High mountain vegetation (high land which is cold and which may have small plants growing)

 Tundra (land near the Arctic which is cold and is covered in small plants, with no trees)

 Oceans, seas and lakes

 City

 Country border

~~~~~ River

The World

This is a map of the world. All the land on Earth is divided into seven large areas called continents. All the sea is divided into four large areas called oceans.

Some important places are named on this map. More places are named on the other maps in this atlas.

The maps in this book start with where we live. Then you will find maps of each continent in turn. Use this world map to find where each continent is in the world.

CANADA

NORTH AMERICA

UNITED STATES OF AMERICA

Rocky Mountains

Mississippi River

New York

ATLANTIC OCEAN

PACIFIC OCEAN

River Amazon

BRAZIL

SOUTH AMERICA

Andes

Buenos Aires

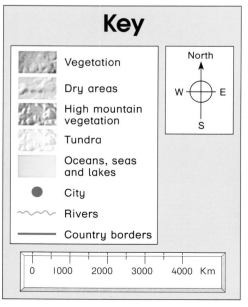

Key

Vegetation	
Dry areas	
High mountain vegetation	
Tundra	
Oceans, seas and lakes	
City	
Rivers	
Country borders	

North
W — E
S

| 0 | 1000 | 2000 | 3000 | 4000 Km |

Animals of the world
The animals at the bottom of each page in this atlas live in different continents. For example, the animals on pages 10 to 19 all live somewhere in Europe. Look on page 47 to find out their names and to find out if they are endangered.

ARCTIC OCEAN

EUROPE

Paris

A F R I C A

AHARA DESERT

Cairo

River Nite

R U S S I A

Moscow

A S I A

Beijing

C H I N A

Himalayas

INDIA

Bombay

PACIFIC OCEAN

The equator
The line through the middle of
this world map is called the
equator. It is an imaginary line
that circles the earth. Countries
near the equator are hotter
than countries further away.

I N D O N E S I A

Equator

INDIAN OCEAN

AUSTRALIA

Sydney

A N T A R C T I C A

The British Isles

The British Isles are made up of two large islands with many small islands dotted around them. They are divided into two parts – the United Kingdom and the Republic of Ireland. Each part has its own parliament. The United Kingdom is made up of Scotland, England, Wales and Northern Ireland.

Rolling hills
Much of England is covered by green, rolling farmland.

Rocky coastline
The coast of Wales is made up of jagged rocks and sandy beaches.

The British Isles
The longest river is the Shannon, in Ireland (386 kilometres long).

The highest mountain is Ben Nevis, in Scotland (1,343 metres high).

The largest lake is Lough Neagh, in Northern Ireland (382 square kilometres).

The deepest cave is Ogof Ffynnon Ddu, in Wales (308 metres deep).

The largest city is London, in England (6,806,000 people).

Ireland

Scotland

Northern Ireland

Wales

England

Key

	Vegetation
	Dry areas
	High mountain vegetation
	Tundra
	Oceans, seas and lakes
●	City
～～	Rivers
──	Country borders

North
W ⊕ E
S

0   50   100   150   200 Km

ATLANTIC OCEAN

SCOTLAND

Edinburgh

Mountains and glens
Scotland has many mountains. Between the mountains are deep valleys called glens.

NORTH SEA

NORTHERN IRELAND

Belfast

U N I T E D

K I N G D O M

River Shannon

Dublin

REPUBLIC OF IRELAND

Snowdonia

River Trent

River Severn

WALES

E N G L A N D

Cardiff

London

River Thames

11

Close-up on Northern Britain

Northern Britain has mountains, moors and lakes. The weather is usually colder than in southern Britain, and more snow falls here than in the south. Farmers raise sheep and cattle on hill farms, and many people work in factories around the big cities.

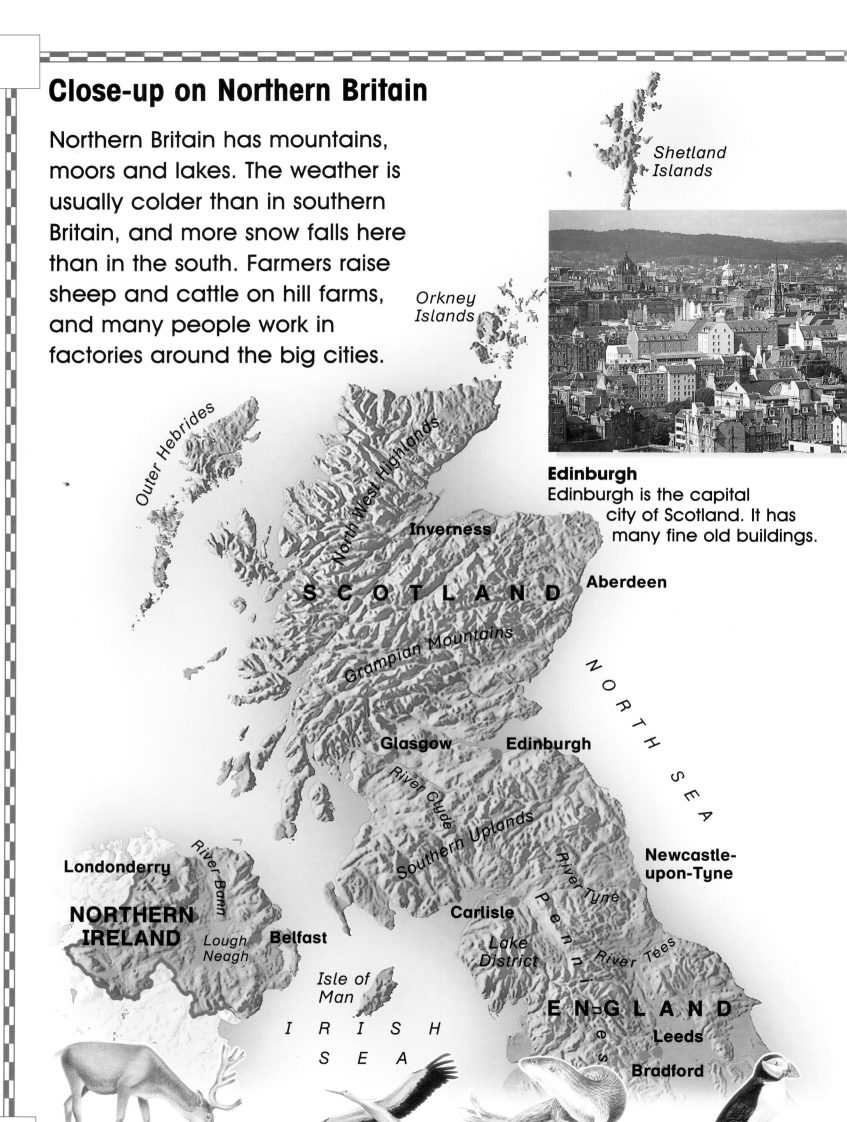

Shetland Islands

Orkney Islands

Edinburgh

Edinburgh
Edinburgh is the capital city of Scotland. It has many fine old buildings.

Outer Hebrides

North West Highlands

Inverness

S C O T L A N D

Aberdeen

Grampian Mountains

Glasgow

Edinburgh

N O R T H   S E A

River Clyde

Southern Uplands

River Tyne

Newcastle-upon-Tyne

NORTHERN IRELAND

Londonderry

River Bann

Lough Neagh

Belfast

Carlisle

Lake District

P e n n i n e s

River Tees

Isle of Man

I R I S H   S E A

E N G L A N D

Leeds

Bradford

Key

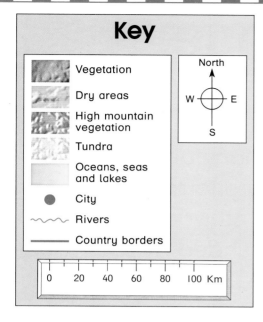

- Vegetation
- Dry areas
- High mountain vegetation
- Tundra
- Oceans, seas and lakes
- ● City
- ～ Rivers
- — Country borders

North
W ✦ E
S

0 20 40 60 80 100 Km

Close-up on Southern Britain

The weather in southern Britain is usually warmer and sunnier than in the north. Farmers in the east mostly grow crops. In the west farmers mostly raise sheep and dairy cows. There are many factories, especially in the centre of England. Many people work in shops and offices in London, the capital city of the United Kingdom.

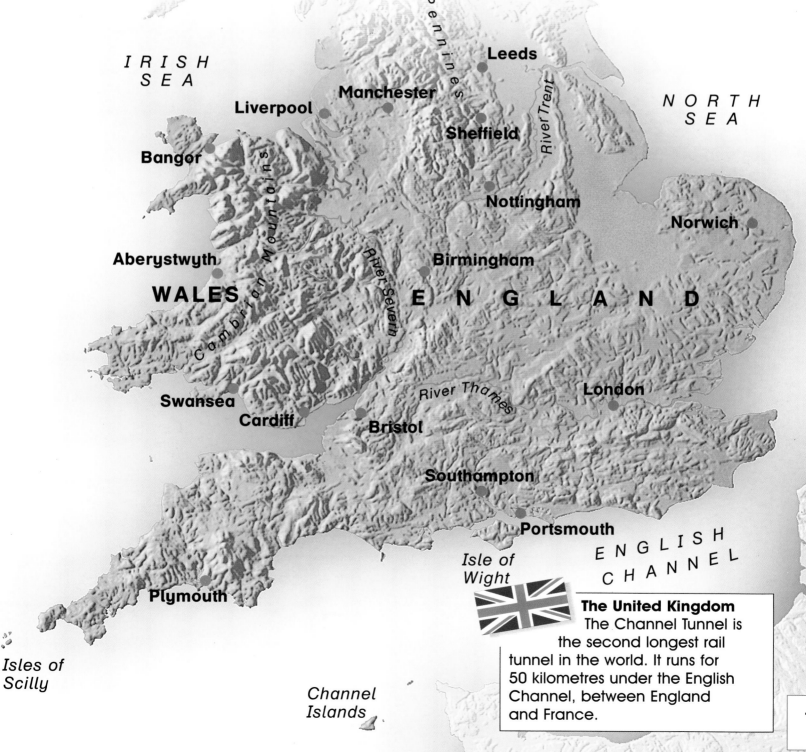

IRISH SEA

NORTH SEA

Pennines

Leeds
Manchester
Liverpool
Bangor
Sheffield
River Trent
Nottingham
Norwich
Cambrian Mountains
Aberystwyth
Birmingham
River Severn
WALES
ENGLAND
River Thames
London
Swansea
Cardiff
Bristol
Southampton
Portsmouth
Isle of Wight
ENGLISH CHANNEL
Plymouth
Isles of Scilly
Channel Islands

The United Kingdom
The Channel Tunnel is the second longest rail tunnel in the world. It runs for 50 kilometres under the English Channel, between England and France.

13

Europe

Europe is a small continent – only Australia is smaller – but many people live there and some parts are very crowded. It is surrounded by sea to the north, south and west but to the east it is joined to Asia. Europe has a ragged coastline, with fingers of land pointing into the sea. The north of Europe is wet and cold, but summers in the south are hot and dry.

Forests in the north
Parts of northern Europe are covered in forests. Reindeer feed on the mosses and lichens that grow on the ground.

A peak in the Alps
The mountains of the Alps run through Switzerland and several other countries. Can you find three of them? Look at the maps on page 15 and page 17.

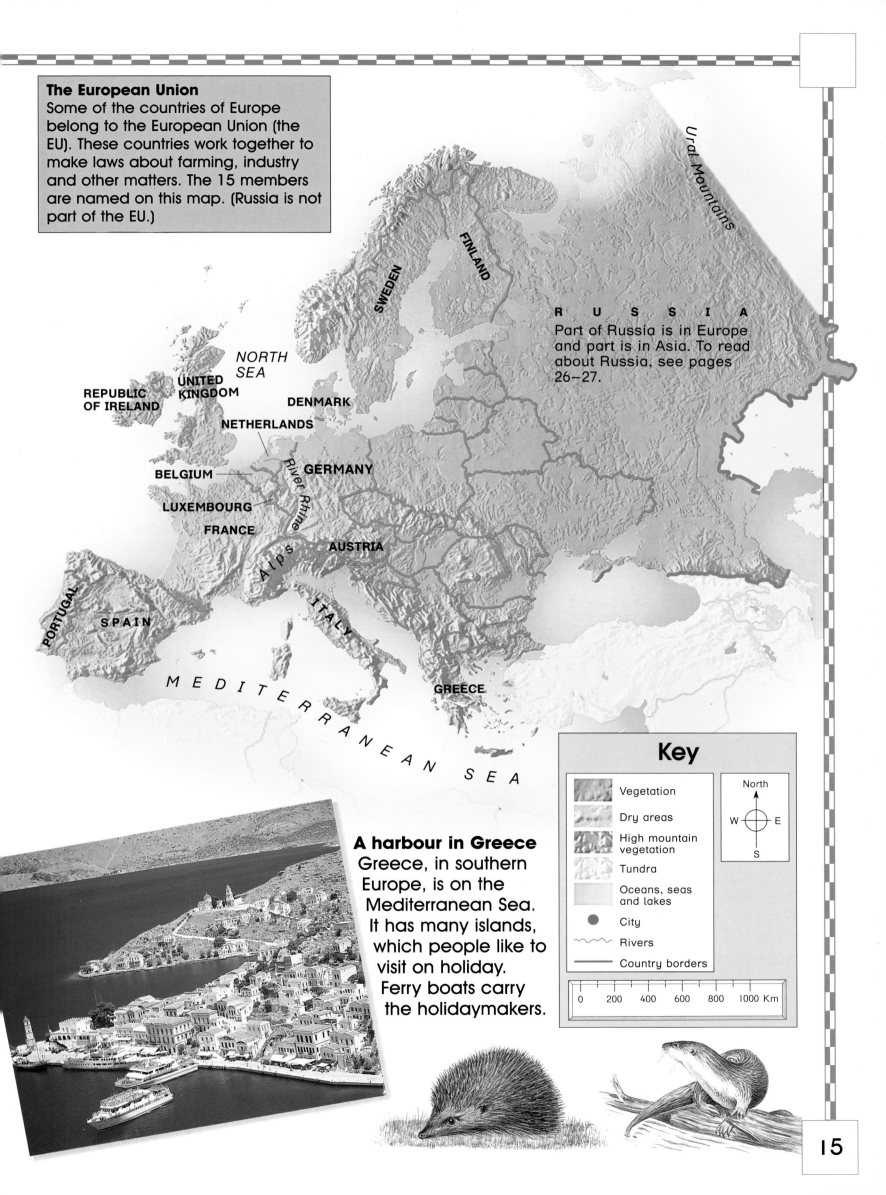

The European Union
Some of the countries of Europe belong to the European Union (the EU). These countries work together to make laws about farming, industry and other matters. The 15 members are named on this map. (Russia is not part of the EU.)

Ural Mountains

SWEDEN

FINLAND

R U S S I A
Part of Russia is in Europe and part is in Asia. To read about Russia, see pages 26–27.

NORTH SEA

REPUBLIC OF IRELAND

UNITED KINGDOM

DENMARK

NETHERLANDS

BELGIUM

River Rhine

GERMANY

LUXEMBOURG

FRANCE

Alps

AUSTRIA

PORTUGAL

SPAIN

ITALY

GREECE

M E D I T E R R A N E A N   S E A

A harbour in Greece
Greece, in southern Europe, is on the Mediterranean Sea. It has many islands, which people like to visit on holiday. Ferry boats carry the holidaymakers.

Key

	Vegetation
	Dry areas
	High mountain vegetation
	Tundra
	Oceans, seas and lakes
●	City
～	Rivers
—	Country borders

North
W — E
S

0   200   400   600   800   1000 Km

Close-up on Northern Europe

The far north of Europe is a very cold land, covered with mountains, lakes and forests of pine trees. Further south the land is flatter and lower, making it good for farming. In the centre of Europe there are many factories. Barges carry coal, wheat and timber along wide rivers.

Fjords in Norway
A fjord is an inlet of sea between steep cliffs. There are many fjords along the coast of Norway.

Germany
For many years, Germany was divided into two countries, East Germany and West Germany. But they joined together again in 1990.

Buses and boats in London
London is the largest city in Europe. The River Thames runs through the city.

The River Rhine
The River Rhine flows through Germany. It carries more shipping than any other river in the world. It also carries pollution from factories along its banks to the North Sea.

Oil in the North Sea

Some oil lies under the sea. Huge drills cut through the rock on the sea bed to reach the oil. The men who drill for oil live on an oil rig.

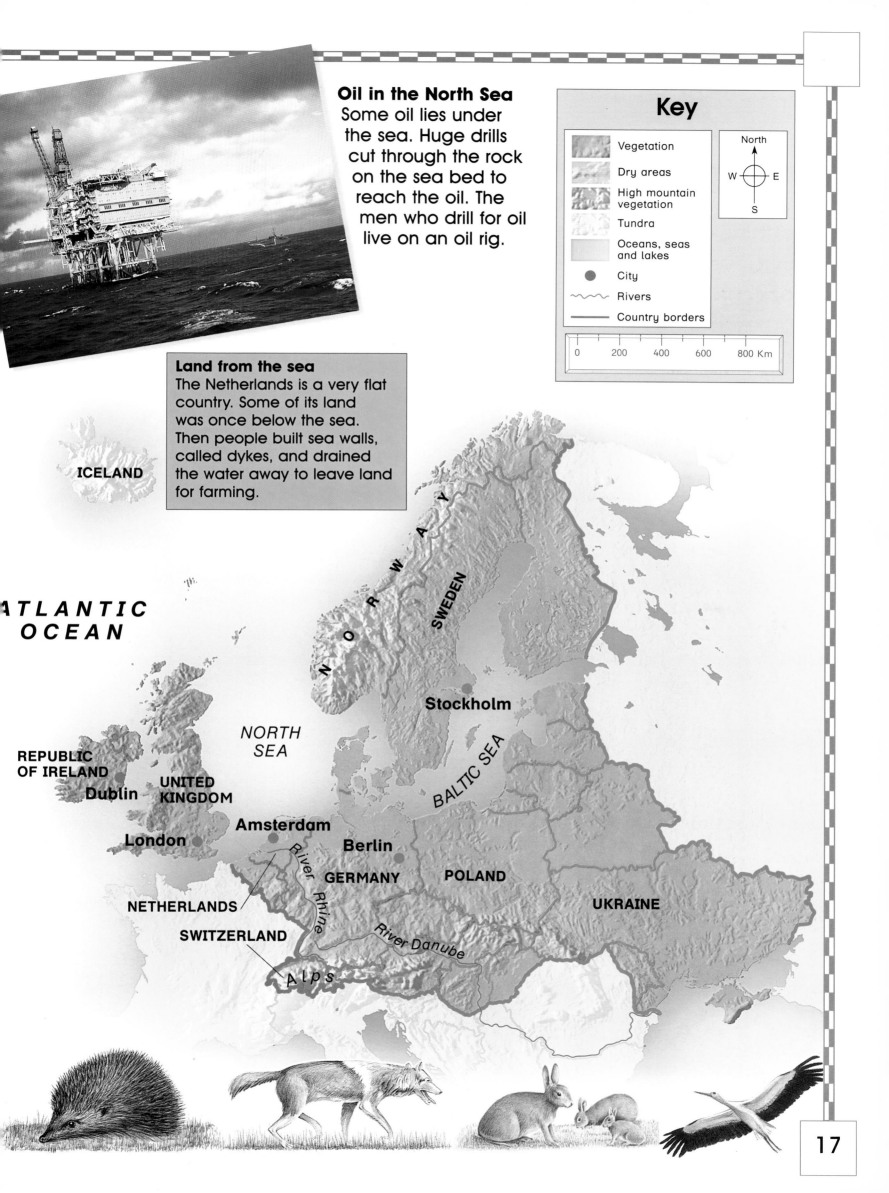

Key

	Vegetation
	Dry areas
	High mountain vegetation
	Tundra
	Oceans, seas and lakes
●	City
～	Rivers
—	Country borders

North
W — E
S

0   200   400   600   800 Km

Land from the sea

The Netherlands is a very flat country. Some of its land was once below the sea. Then people built sea walls, called dykes, and drained the water away to leave land for farming.

ICELAND

ATLANTIC
OCEAN

N O R W A Y

SWEDEN

Stockholm

NORTH SEA

BALTIC SEA

REPUBLIC OF IRELAND

Dublin

UNITED KINGDOM

Amsterdam

London

Berlin

River Rhine

GERMANY

POLAND

UKRAINE

NETHERLANDS

SWITZERLAND

River Danube

A l p s

Close-up on Southern Europe

Southern Europe is protected from the cold winds of the north by two large mountain chains – the Alps and the Pyrenees. Fruits such as grapes and oranges grow well here and many people are farmers. Tourists stay by the Mediterrranean Sea in summer, and ski in the mountains in winter.

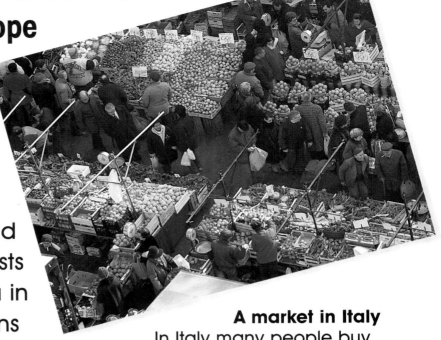

A market in Italy
In Italy many people buy their food fresh every day from street markets. Tomatoes, oranges and lemons grow well in the hot, dry summers.

France
France is the third largest country in Europe (after Russia and Ukraine). It has the deepest cave in the world, the Réseau Jean Bernard. It is 1,602 metres deep – deep enough to fit Ben Nevis inside! (See page 10.)

Vatican City
St Peter's Square in Rome, Italy, is part of a tiny country called Vatican City. This is the home of the Pope, the head of the Roman Catholic Church.

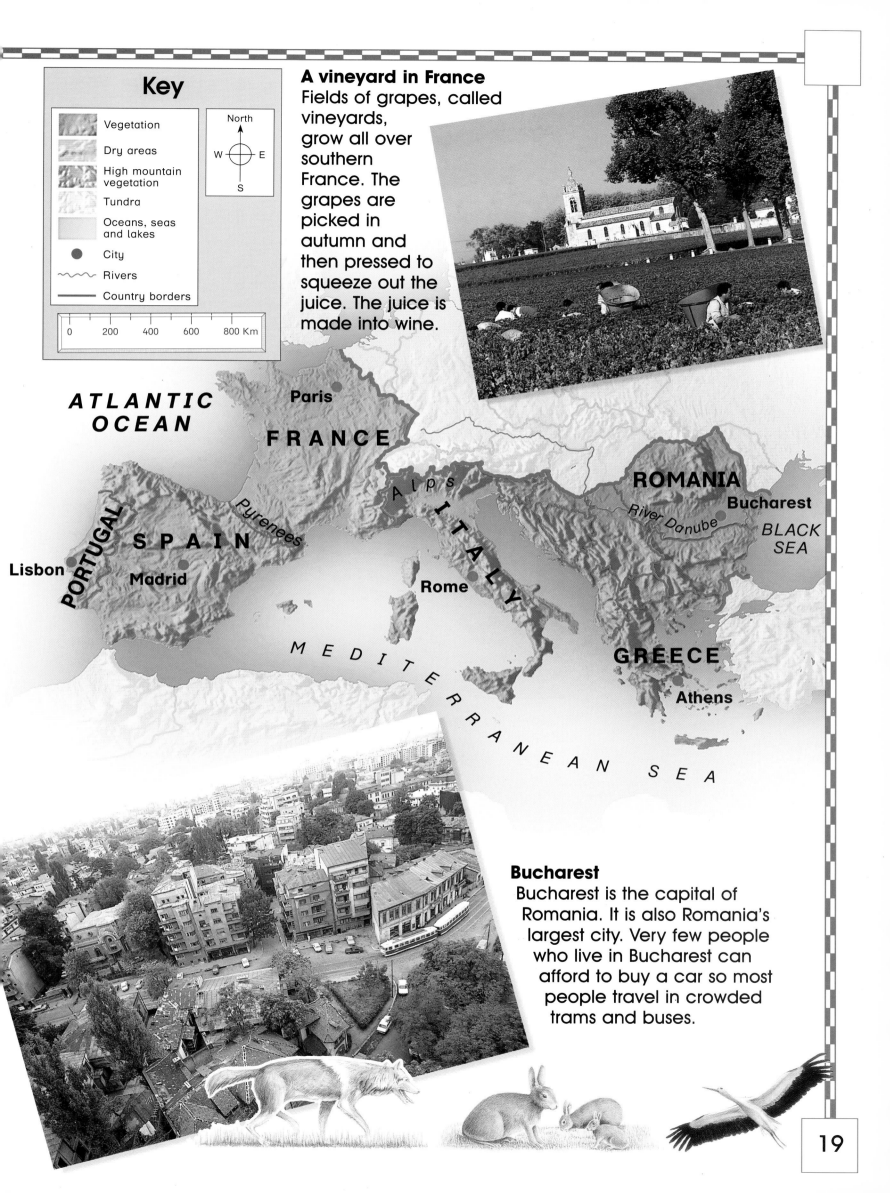

Key

	Vegetation
	Dry areas
	High mountain vegetation
	Tundra
	Oceans, seas and lakes
●	City
∿	Rivers
—	Country borders

North
W — E
S

0   200   400   600   800 Km

A vineyard in France

Fields of grapes, called vineyards, grow all over southern France. The grapes are picked in autumn and then pressed to squeeze out the juice. The juice is made into wine.

ATLANTIC OCEAN

Paris

FRANCE

Alps

ROMANIA

Bucharest

River Danube

BLACK SEA

PORTUGAL

Pyrenees

S P A I N

ITALY

Lisbon

Madrid

Rome

M E D I T E R R A N E A N   S E A

GREECE

Athens

Bucharest

Bucharest is the capital of Romania. It is also Romania's largest city. Very few people who live in Bucharest can afford to buy a car so most people travel in crowded trams and buses.

Africa

Africa is the second largest continent in the world. It has mountains, hot deserts, thick rainforests and large, flat grasslands called the savannah. The Nile is the longest river in the world and the Sahara is the largest desert. Elephants, zebras and giraffes live in Africa.

Deserts
Deserts are very dry places, with little or no rain. Deserts can be either hot or cold. Some of Africa is covered in large, hot deserts.

Dunes in the desert
Along the southwest coast of Africa runs the Namib Desert. It has huge sand dunes.

African elephants
The African elephant is the biggest land animal in the world. It eats grass, twigs and bark. Many elephants are killed for their ivory tusks.

Great Rift Valley

The Great Rift Valley in east Africa is a huge crack in the Earth's surface. There are many lakes, swamps and volcanoes. Can you see a volcano with its crater in this picture?

Rainforests

Central Africa is covered in thick rainforest. It is always hot and rainy. The great River Zaire flows through the rainforest.

Sailing on the Nile

Boats with triangle-shaped sails have been used on the River Nile for hundreds of years.

Tanzania

The highest mountain in Africa is Kilimanjaro, in Tanzania. It is 5,895 metres high. Its name means the mountain that glitters, because the peak is always covered in ice.

Close-up on Africa

Many different peoples live in Africa. Some work in large cities, but many others are nomads or farmers and are very poor. Africa's savannah often suffers from drought and the people who live there are forced to move in search of food, water and farmland.

South Africa
The deepest mine in the world is a gold mine in South Africa. It is 3,777 metres deep. It is so hot down there that refrigerators are used to keep the air cool!

Taking the load
Many women in Africa walk many miles each day to fetch water and find wood for fuel. They carry their loads on their heads.

Skyscrapers in Nairobi
Nairobi is the capital city of Kenya. It has many tall office blocks and factories.

Digging for gold
This gold mine is in South Africa. The men are working nearly two kilometres below ground.

Water in the desert

Nomads are people who move from place to place to find food and water. These nomads are in Sudan. They are collecting water from a well in animal skins.

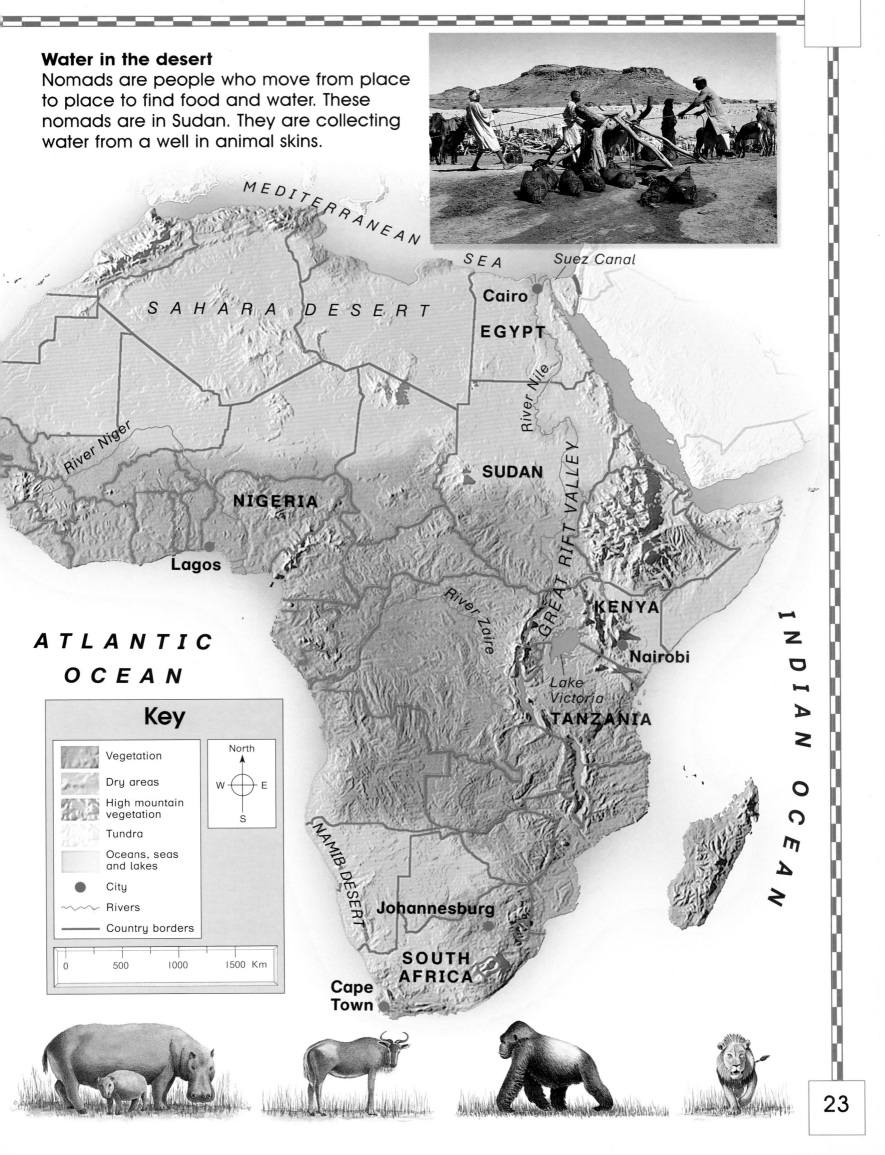

MEDITERRANEAN

SEA

Suez Canal

SAHARA DESERT

Cairo

EGYPT

River Nile

River Niger

SUDAN

NIGERIA

Lagos

River Zaire

GREAT RIFT VALLEY

KENYA

ATLANTIC
OCEAN

Nairobi

Lake
Victoria

TANZANIA

INDIAN OCEAN

Key

	Vegetation
	Dry areas
	High mountain vegetation
	Tundra
	Oceans, seas and lakes
●	City
~~	Rivers
——	Country borders

North

W ← → E

S

0	500	1000	1500 Km

NAMIB DESERT

Johannesburg

SOUTH
AFRICA

Cape
Town

23

Asia

Asia is the largest continent in the world. It has hot and cold deserts, thick forests and many high mountains. Mount Everest in the Himalayas is the highest mountain in the world, and the Caspian Sea is the largest lake. More than half the world's people live in Asia.

Muddy river
The Hwang Ho is the second longest river in China. It is called the Yellow River in English, because of the colour of the mud it carries.

Rainforest riches
The rainforest in Malaysia is home to many beautiful plants and animals. But the forest is being cut down for mining and for rubber plantations.

Life in the mountains

The yak is very important to the people of Nepal, in the Himalayas. It doesn't mind the cold, it carries heavy loads, and provides milk and wool.

Life in the desert

Water holes like this one in the desert in Saudi Arabia provide water for plants to grow and people and animals to drink.

Nomads in China

Cattle and sheep graze on the grasslands in China. The farmers will move their animals on when the grass is gone.

Monsoon rains

Farmers in southern Asia rely on heavy rains each summer to make their crops grow. The strong wind that brings the rains is called the monsoon.

Monsoon rains in India

Israel and Jordan

The Dead Sea is on the border between Israel and Jordan. It is the lowest place on earth – 396 metres below sea level. The water is very, very salty, which makes it easy to float in.

Russia and Northern Asia

Russia is the largest country in the world and crosses both Europe and Asia. Most of Russia's people live in the west, which is in Europe. The eastern part is called Siberia. Here it is very cold for most of the year. In the south are the flat grassy steppes, where wheat and other crops are grown.

Haymaking in Mongolia
Grass is cut in summer and dried to make hay. The hay is winter food for the animals. In many parts of the world, children have to help with farming and other work.

A

Pollution in Russia
The air over this street in St Petersburg, in Russia, is polluted with factory fumes.

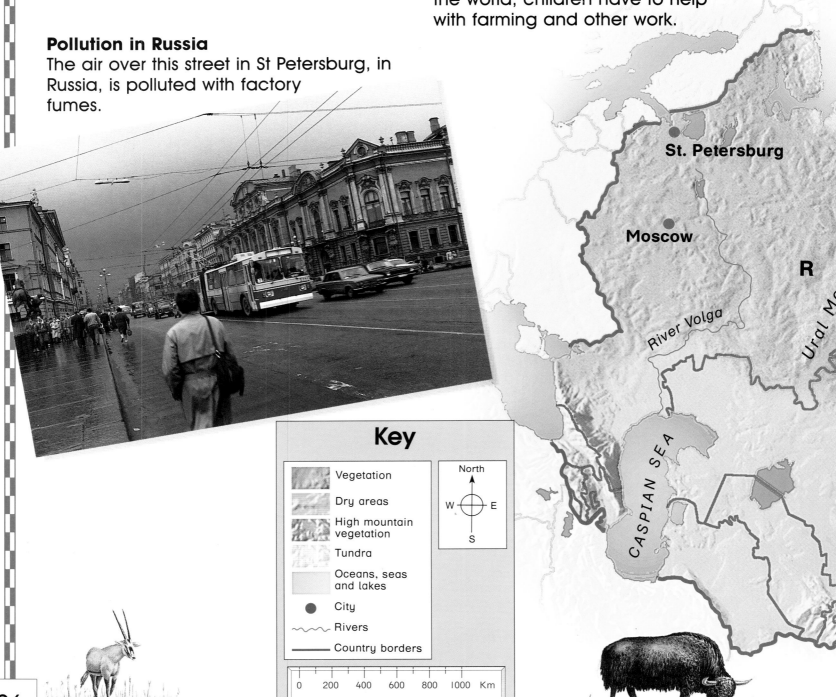

St. Petersburg

Moscow

R

River Volga

Ural Mo

CASPIAN SEA

Key

	Vegetation
	Dry areas
	High mountain vegetation
	Tundra
	Oceans, seas and lakes
●	City
〜〜	Rivers
—	Country borders

North
W — E
S

0 200 400 600 800 1000 Km

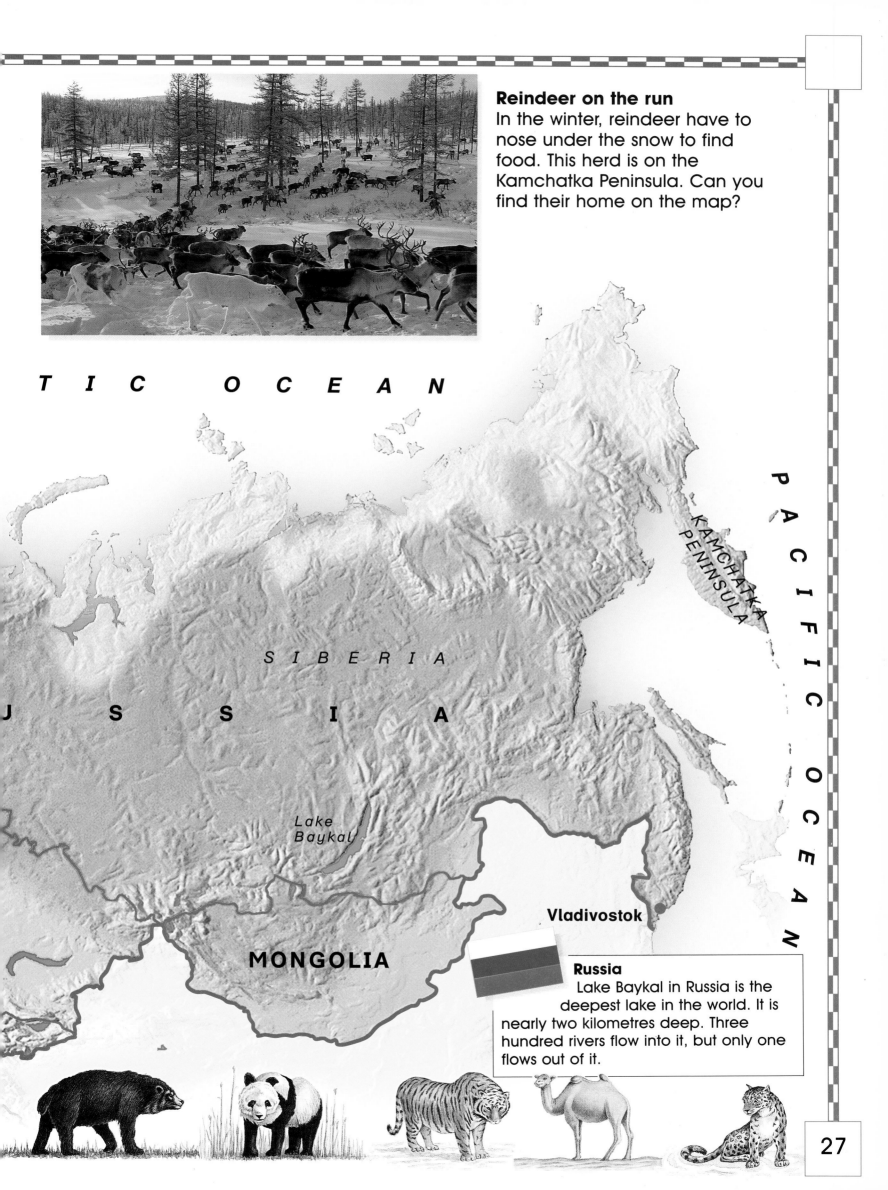

Reindeer on the run
In the winter, reindeer have to nose under the snow to find food. This herd is on the Kamchatka Peninsula. Can you find their home on the map?

TIC OCEAN

PACIFIC OCEAN

KAMCHATKA PENINSULA

SIBERIA

USSIA

Lake Baykal

Vladivostok

MONGOLIA

Russia
Lake Baykal in Russia is the deepest lake in the world. It is nearly two kilometres deep. Three hundred rivers flow into it, but only one flows out of it.

27

India and Southern Asia

In the west, where Asia meets Africa, is an area called the Middle East. Most of the land here is hot desert. Huge amounts of oil have been found in the desert and out at sea, which has made some countries very rich. In India, to the east, many people are very poor. They live in crowded cities along the coast and along rivers.

Tea pickers
Women in Bangladesh carry the tea they have picked in large baskets on their heads.

India
The wettest place in the world is Mawsynram in northeast India. On average, nearly 12 metres of rain fall every year.

Rivers and deltas
When a large river reaches the sea it sometimes splits up into smaller rivers, making a delta. Land near deltas is often flooded. Bangladesh is flooded by the Ganges delta.

Calcutta
Calcutta's busy streets are crowded with carts, cars and bicycles. More than 11 million people live there. It is one of the most crowded places in the world.

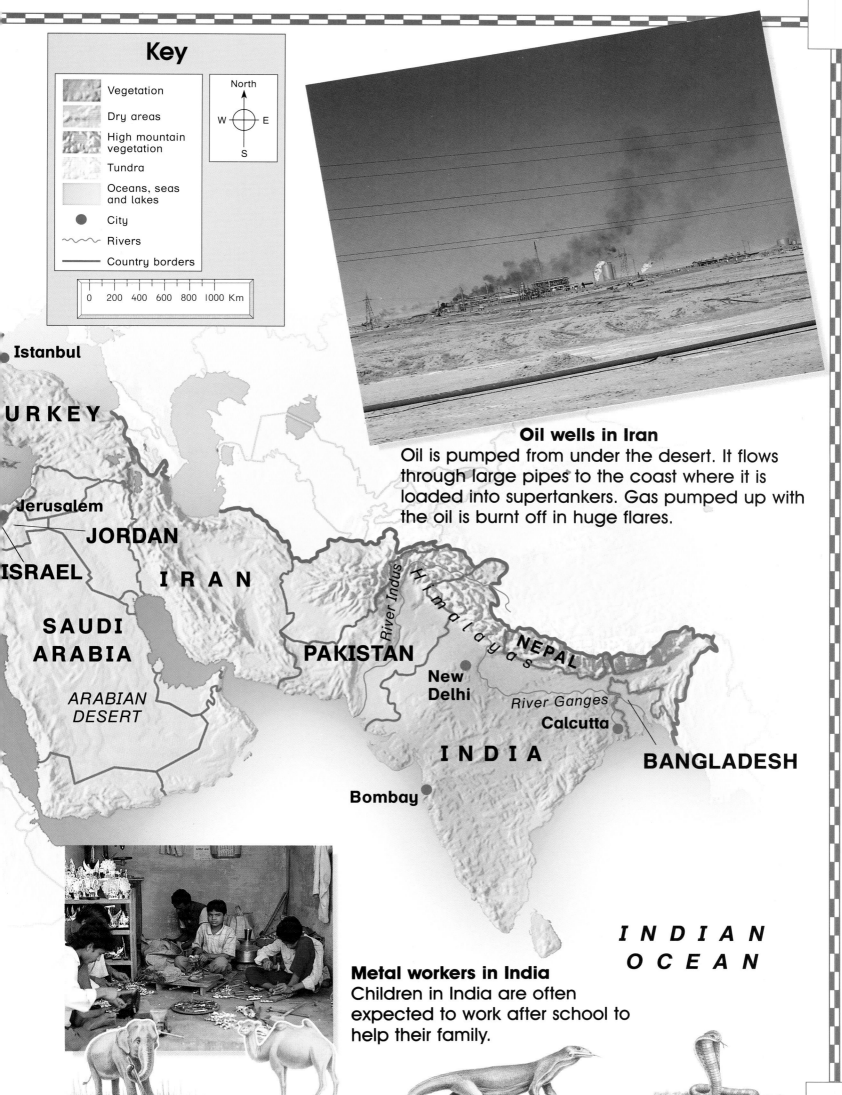

Key

	Vegetation
	Dry areas
	High mountain vegetation
	Tundra
	Oceans, seas and lakes
●	City
∿	Rivers
—	Country borders

North
W ← ⊕ → E
S

0 200 400 600 800 1000 Km

Istanbul

TURKEY

Jerusalem

JORDAN

ISRAEL

IRAN

SAUDI ARABIA

ARABIAN DESERT

River Indus

Himalayas

PAKISTAN

NEPAL

New Delhi

River Ganges

Calcutta

BANGLADESH

INDIA

Bombay

INDIAN OCEAN

Oil wells in Iran
Oil is pumped from under the desert. It flows through large pipes to the coast where it is loaded into supertankers. Gas pumped up with the oil is burnt off in huge flares.

Metal workers in India
Children in India are often expected to work after school to help their family.

China and Eastern Asia

More people live in China than in any other country in the world. It is a huge country – almost as big as the whole of Europe. Japan is a very rich country with crowded cities and towns. In Southeast Asia, the forests are being cut down for their fine wood and to make room for more farmland.

Japan's capital city

Tokyo is one of the biggest cities in the world. It is so large it is sometimes called a megalopolis, which means 'great city'. In this picture you can see Mount Fuji in the background.

Rice fields

Rice is grown all over this region. It is often grown in fields cut into the mountain side.

G O B I   D E S E R T

Beijing

Tokyo

JAPAN

Hwang Ho

Chang Jiang

C H I N A

PACIFIC OCEAN

Hong Kong

Mekong

M A L A Y S I A

I N D O N E S I A

Millions of bicycles
The main way of getting around in China is by bicycle. If everyone had cars, as they do in the West, the traffic jams would be enormous!

Indonesia
 The country of Indonesia is made up of more than 13,000 islands. Only about half have people living on them. Because the people are so spread out, Indonesia has more than 250 different languages.

Earthquakes
Sometimes rocks underground move. They push against each other and break. This makes the ground shake and huge cracks may appear. This is called an earthquake. Many earthquakes happen in Japan.

Oceania

Oceania is made up of Australia, New Zealand and many other islands in the Pacific Ocean. Australia is the world's smallest continent. It is very flat and dry. New Zealand is wetter and has many mountains. The Pacific is the largest and deepest ocean in the world. It is dotted with islands made by volcanoes.

Volcanoes
Volcanoes are mountains made from ash and lava. Lava is hot, boiling rock which pours out from inside the Earth when a volcano erupts.

Great Barrier Reef
Australia's Great Barrier Reef is a long chain of coral. Tourists and divers visit the reef to see the many types of brightly coloured fish that live there.

Hot, dusty desert
The middle of Australia is covered by large deserts. It is hot and dry in the daytime and cold at night. Very few people live here.

Australia
The Great Barrier Reef, on Australia's northeast coast, is the largest structure made by a living thing. It is 2,028 kilometres long. It is made of coral which is formed by tiny animals.

Coral islands
Most countries in the Pacific Ocean are made up of groups of tiny coral islands. No one lives on the smallest islands.

New Zealand's rainforests
A lot of New Zealand is warm and wet all year round. Rainforests grow here. Many of the plants are not found anywhere else in the world.

Australia and New Zealand

Australia is a big country, but not many people live there. In the middle is desert, called the outback. Australia is so dry that it is difficult to grow crops, so farmers raise cows and sheep on huge farms. Sheep farming is important in New Zealand, too. New Zealand is made up of two islands. It has volcanoes and hot springs called geysers.

Aborigines
The girl on the right of this picture is an Aborigine. The Aborigines were the first people to live in Australia. Today, most Australians have European ancestors, like the girl on the left.

Sydney
Sydney is the oldest and largest city in Australia. Its world-famous Opera House is shown on the left of this picture. Most Australians live on the coast in cities like Sydney.

The Flying Doctors
Doctors must travel by plane to reach patients who live on huge cattle ranches and sheep farms in the outback. The farms are so far apart that travelling by car would take too long.

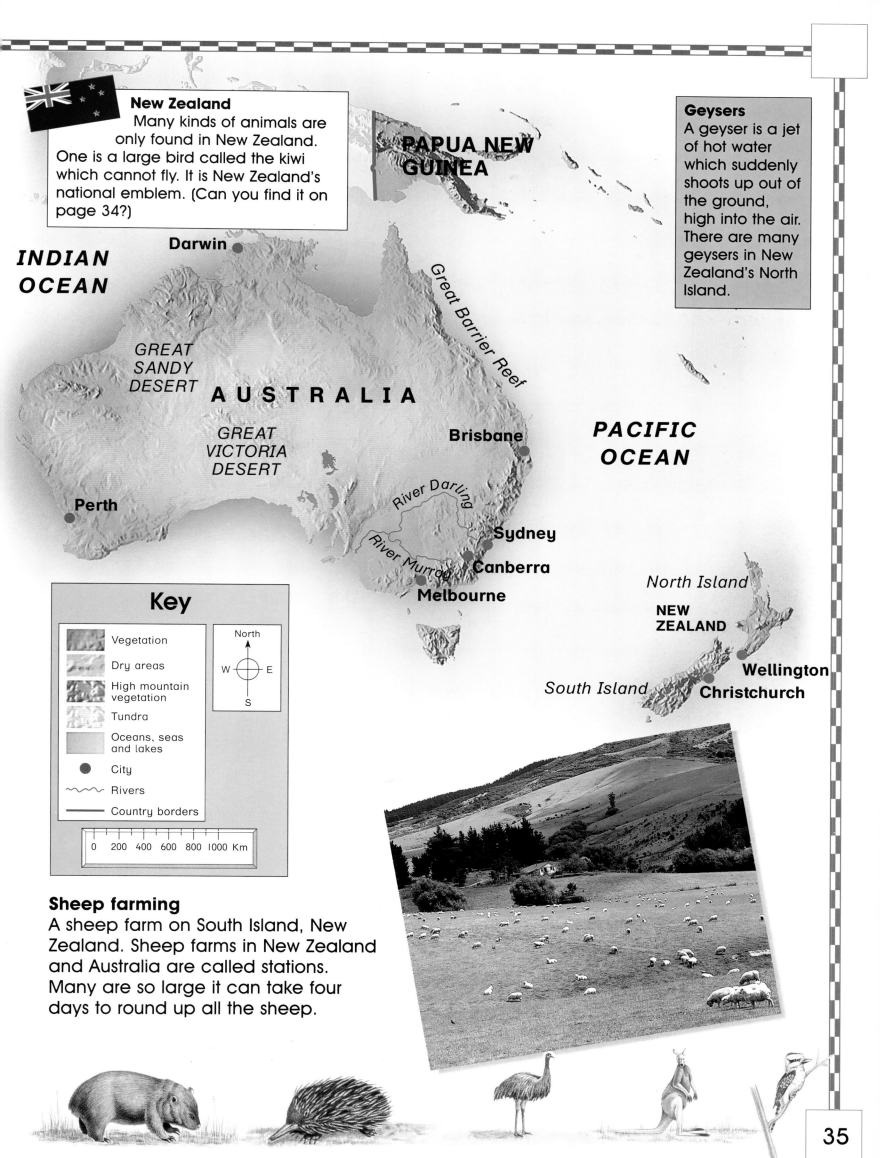

New Zealand
Many kinds of animals are only found in New Zealand. One is a large bird called the kiwi which cannot fly. It is New Zealand's national emblem. (Can you find it on page 34?)

Geysers
A geyser is a jet of hot water which suddenly shoots up out of the ground, high into the air. There are many geysers in New Zealand's North Island.

PAPUA NEW GUINEA

INDIAN OCEAN

Darwin

GREAT SANDY DESERT

AUSTRALIA

GREAT VICTORIA DESERT

Great Barrier Reef

PACIFIC OCEAN

Perth

Brisbane

River Darling

River Murray

Sydney

Canberra

Melbourne

North Island

NEW ZEALAND

South Island

Wellington

Christchurch

Key

Vegetation

Dry areas

High mountain vegetation

Tundra

Oceans, seas and lakes

● City

∿ Rivers

— Country borders

North
W E
S

0 200 400 600 800 1000 Km

Sheep farming
A sheep farm on South Island, New Zealand. Sheep farms in New Zealand and Australia are called stations. Many are so large it can take four days to round up all the sheep.

North America

North America is the third largest continent. In the north it is cold and snowy, and there are many mountains, lakes, rivers and forests. In the south there are deserts and rainforests. In the middle are the Great Plains, a huge area of flat grassland. Strung out into the Caribbean Sea is a chain of tropical islands, which are sometimes hit by hurricanes.

Canada
Canada has the longest coastline of any country in the world. If it was stretched out straight, it would go round the world six times. Canada also has more than one million lakes.

Mountain forests
The Rocky Mountains run all the way down the western side of North America. In Canada the slopes are covered with thick forests of pine trees.

Storm struck island

The islands of the Caribbean are struck by hurricanes every year. The strong winds can blow trees down and sometimes people are killed.

Hurricanes

A hurricane is a violent storm with very strong winds. It can cause a lot of damage. Hurricanes often blow up in the Caribbean Sea.

Thundering waterfall

Niagara Falls is a group of huge waterfalls between Canada and the United States of America. The water pouring over them comes from the Great Lakes.

Desert canyon

This deep valley is the Grand Canyon in the United States. It was made by the River Colorado as it cut through the desert.

Close-up on North America

North America has two very large countries, Canada and the United States of America. Both countries have modern factories, large farms and busy cities. The United States is one of the richest countries in the world.

Native Americans
The first people to live in North America were the Native Americans. This man is wearing traditional dress for a special occasion.

The United States of America
The sunniest place in the world is Yuma, in Arizona. On average, the sun shines for 11 hours a day. But the hottest place in the world may be Death Valley in California. Temperatures here can reach above 49°C.

Wheat fields
Wheat is grown in huge fields on the flat open prairies of Canada and the United States.

New York
New York is the largest city in the United States. Some of the world's tallest skyskrapers line its busy streets.

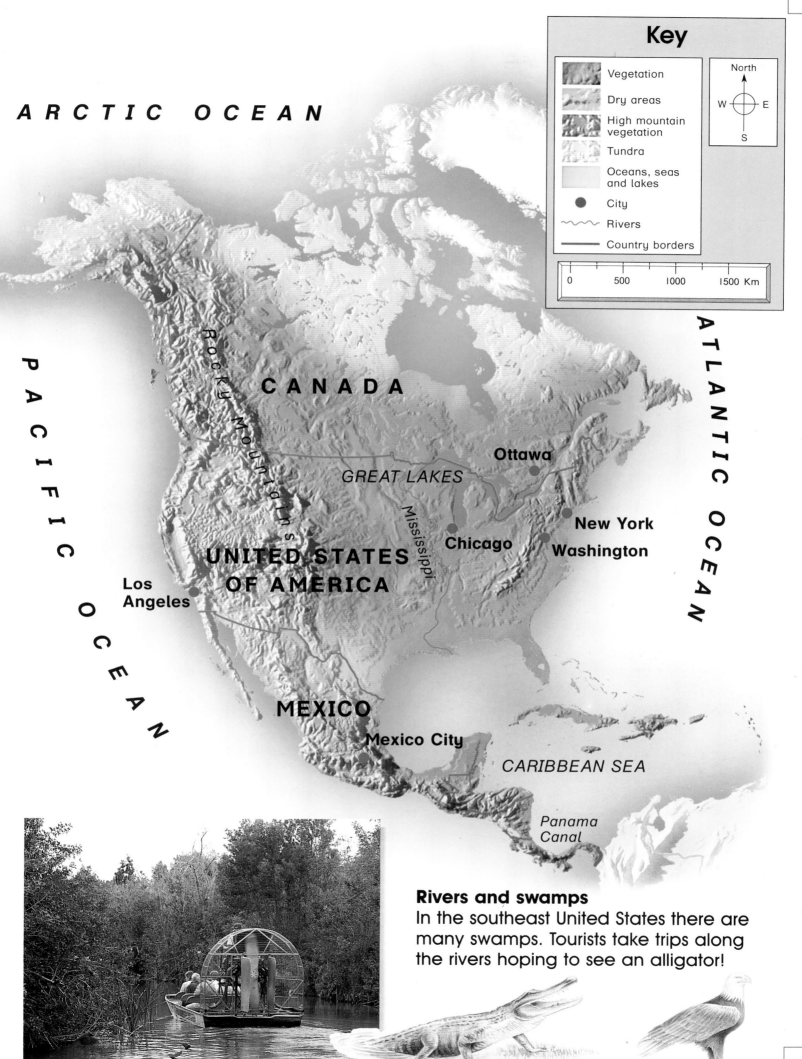

ARCTIC OCEAN

PACIFIC OCEAN

ATLANTIC OCEAN

Key

- Vegetation
- Dry areas
- High mountain vegetation
- Tundra
- Oceans, seas and lakes
- ● City
- ～ Rivers
- — Country borders

North
W ⊕ E
S

| 0 | 500 | 1000 | 1500 Km |

CANADA

Rocky Mountains

GREAT LAKES

Ottawa

Mississippi

Chicago

New York

Washington

UNITED STATES
OF AMERICA

Los
Angeles

MEXICO

Mexico City

CARIBBEAN SEA

Panama
Canal

Rivers and swamps
In the southeast United States there are many swamps. Tourists take trips along the rivers hoping to see an alligator!

South America

South America is the fourth largest continent. It has hot and cold deserts, high mountains, thick rainforests and grassy plains. The Atacama Desert is the driest place in the world and the Andes is the longest chain of mountains. The River Amazon flows through the world's largest rainforest.

The mighty Amazon
The River Amazon is huge. It carries more water than any other river in the world. It flows through Peru and Brazil from the Andes to the Atlantic Ocean.

Venezuela
Angel Falls in Venezuela is the highest waterfall in the world. It is 979 metres high, which is three times as tall as the Eiffel Tower in Paris, France.

Losing a home
The rainforest in Brazil is being cut down or burned to make room for farming and mining. But animals like this tamarin monkey are becoming rare as their home is destroyed.

A long line of peaks
The Andes Mountains run through seven countries in South America. This picture shows the Andes in Peru.

Rainforest
Most rainforests grow in hot wet places near the equator. The rainforest in Brazil is bigger than all the other rainforests in the world put together. More than half of all the plants and animals in the world live in rainforests.

No water
It is easy to see why this is called the Valley of the Moon, in the Atacama Desert, in Chile. In 1971, rain fell in parts of the desert for the first time in 400 years. In some places, rain has never been recorded.

Close-up on South America

The largest country in South America is Brazil. Much of Brazil is covered by the Amazon rainforest. South America has oil fields, rubber plantations, mines and huge areas of rich farmland, but many people live in crowded cities and are very poor.

Brazil
More sugar cane is grown in the world than any other food crop. And more sugar cane is grown in Brazil than in any other country in the world. Some of the sugar cane is made into a fuel for cars because it is cheaper than petrol.

A city by the sea
Rio de Janeiro is the main port of Brazil. It is one of the biggest cities in the world. In the background is Sugar Loaf Mountain.

On the farm
Sheep and cattle graze on the grasslands in Argentina. The grasslands are called the pampas. The animals are looked after by cowboys, called gauchos.

Life in the city
This is a shanty town in Sao Paulo, in Brazil. A shanty is a hut made of old wood and scrap metal. Many poor people live in shanty towns.

CARIBBEAN SEA

Caracas

VENEZUELA

ATLANTIC OCEAN

River Amazon

B R A Z I L

Andes

P E R U

Lima

Brasilia

PACIFIC OCEAN

Sao Paulo

Rio de Janeiro

C H I L E
ATACAMA DESERT
Andes

A R G E N T I N A

Buenos Aires

Key

	Vegetation
	Dry areas
	High mountain vegetation
	Tundra
	Oceans, seas and lakes
●	City
～～	Rivers
—	Country borders

North
W · E
S

0 200 400 600 800 1000 Km

Life in the rainforest
These boys live in a village in the Amazon rainforest. They live by a river.

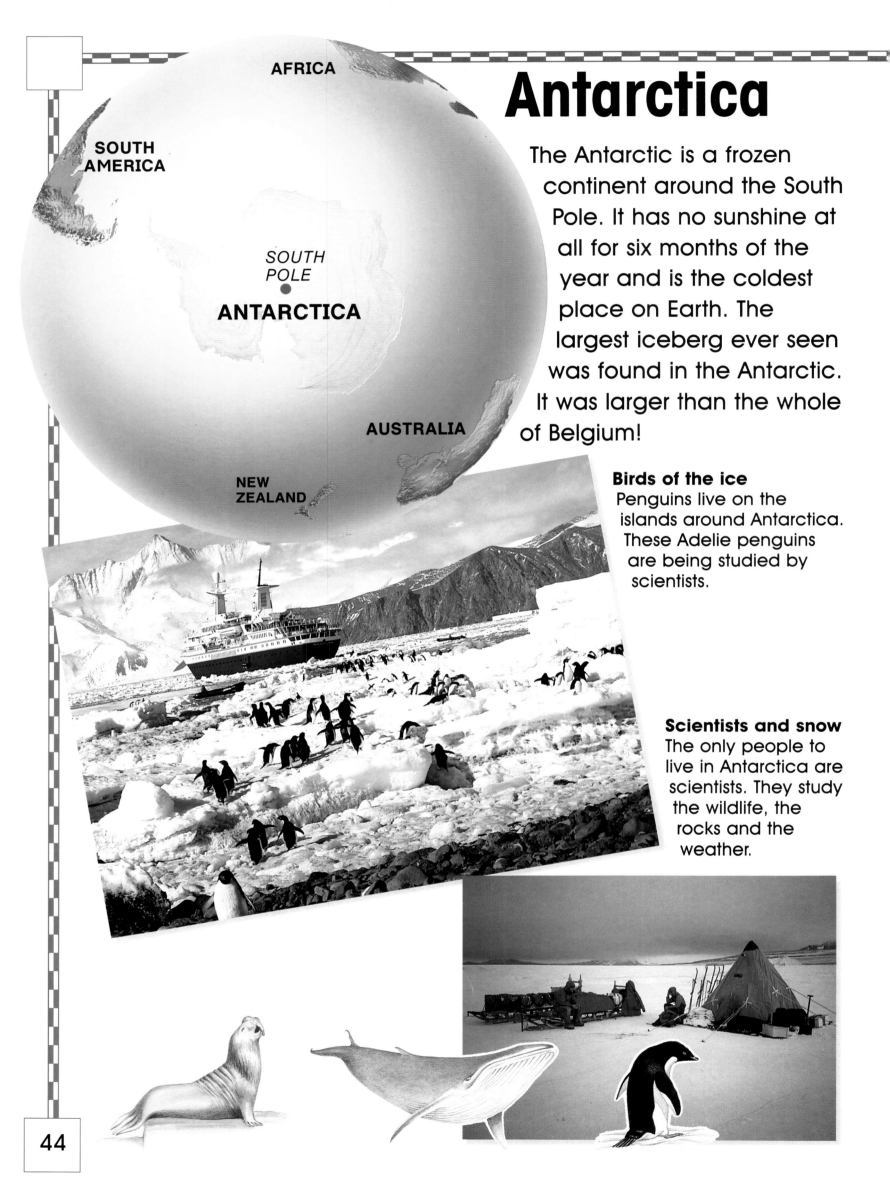

Antarctica

The Antarctic is a frozen continent around the South Pole. It has no sunshine at all for six months of the year and is the coldest place on Earth. The largest iceberg ever seen was found in the Antarctic. It was larger than the whole of Belgium!

Birds of the ice
Penguins live on the islands around Antarctica. These Adelie penguins are being studied by scientists.

Scientists and snow
The only people to live in Antarctica are scientists. They study the wildlife, the rocks and the weather.

AFRICA

SOUTH AMERICA

SOUTH POLE

ANTARCTICA

AUSTRALIA

NEW ZEALAND

Arctic

The frozen sea and ice covered area around the North Pole is called the Arctic. Although it is very cold, many people and animals live on its edges.

NORTH AMERICA

ARCTIC

NORTH POLE

ASIA

OCEAN

GREENLAND

EUROPE

Icebergs
The sea round the North and South Poles is so cold, it freezes. It forms large pieces of floating ice, called icebergs. Only one tenth of an iceberg sits above the water – the rest is hidden under the sea.

Polar bears
Polar bears live on the Arctic ice in summer.

Fishermen in the Arctic
The Arctic Ocean is rich in fish. These boats have taken their catch back to Greenland.

Index

Numbers in **bold** show you where you will find information about the entry. Plain numbers show you where you will find the place marked on a map.

Africa 9, **20–23**, 23, **28**, 44
Alps, mountains **14**, 15, 17, **18**, 19
Amazon rainforest 42
Amazon, River 8, **40**, 43
Amsterdam 17
Andes, mountains 8, **40**, **41**, 43
Antarctic 8–9, **44**, 44
Arabian Desert 29
Arctic Ocean 8–9, 27, **45**, 45
Argentina **42**, 43
Asia 9, **14**, **24–31**, 26–27, 29, 30–31, 45
Atacama Desert **40**, **41**, 43
Athens 19
Atlantic Ocean 8–9, 11, 17, 19, 23, 39, **40**, 43
atlas 4, **7**
Australia 9, **32–35**, 35, 44
Austria 15

Baltic Sea 17
Bangladesh **28**, 29
Baykal, Lake **27**, 27
Beijing 9, 31
Belfast 11, 12
Belgium 15
Berlin 17
Black Sea 19
Bombay 9, 29
Brasilia 43
Brazil 8, **40–43**, 43
Brisbane 35
British Isles **10–13**, 11
Bucharest **19**, 19
Buenos Aires 8, 43

Cairo 9, 23
Calcutta **28**, 29
Canada 8, **36–39**, 39
Canberra 35
Cape Town 23
Caracas 43
Cardiff 11, 13
Caribbean Sea **36**, **37**, 39, 43
Caspian Sea 24, 26
Chang Jiang, river 31
Chicago 39
Chile **41**, 43
China 9, **24**, **25**, **30–31**, 31
Christchurch 35
Colorado, River 37
continents 8–9
   see also Africa, Antarctic, Asia, Australia, Europe, North America, South America

Danube, River 17, 19
Darling, River 35

Darwin 35
Dead Sea **25**
delta **28**
Denmark 15
deserts **20**
   see also Arabian, Atacama, Gobi, Great Sandy, Great Victoria, Namib, Sahara
Dublin 11, 17

earthquake **31**
Edinburgh 11, **12**, 12
Egypt 23
England **10**, 10–13, **13**
equator **9**, 9, **41**
Europe 9, **14–19**, 14, 17, 19, **26**, 45
European Union **15**
Everest, Mount **24**

Finland **15**
France 15, **18**, **19**, 19
Fuji, Mount **30**

Ganges, River 29
Germany 15, **16**, 17
geysers **35**
globes **5**
Gobi Desert 31
Grand Canyon **37**
Great Barrier Reef **32**, **33**, 35
Great Lakes **37**, 39
Great Rift Valley **21**, 23
Great Sandy Desert 35
Great Victoria Desert 35
Greece **15**, 15, 19
Greenland **45**, 45

Himalayas, mountains 9, **24**, **25**, 29, 30–31
Hong Kong 31
hurricanes **36**, **37**
Hwang Ho (Yellow River) **24**, 31

iceberg **44**, **45**
Iceland 17
India 9, **28–29**, 29
Indian Ocean 9, 23, 29, 35
Indonesia 9, **31**, 31
Indus, River 29
Iran **29**, 29
Ireland, Republic of **10**, 11, 15, 17
Israel **25**, 29
Istanbul 29
Italy 15, **18**, 19

Japan **30**, 31
Jerusalem 29
Johannesburg 23

Jordan **25**, 29

Kamchatka Peninsula **27**, 27
Kenya 22, 23
key, map **7**
Kilimanjaro, Mount **21**

Lagos 23
Lima 43
Lisbon 19
London **10**, 11, 13, **16**, 17
Los Angeles 39
Luxembourg 15

Madrid 19
Malaysia 24, 31
maps
   how they are made **4–5**
   key **7**
   using **6–7**
   world map **8–9**
Mediterranean Sea 15, **18**, 19, 23
Mekong, river 31
Melbourne 35
Mexico 39
Mexico City 39
Middle East **28**
Mississippi, River 8, 39
Mongolia **26**, 27
monsoon **25**
Moscow 9, 26
Murray, River 35

Nairobi **22**, 23
Namib Desert **20**, 23
Nepal **25**, 29
Netherlands 15, **17**, 17
New Delhi 29
New Zealand **32–35**, 35, 44
New York 8, **38**, 39
Niagara Falls **37**
Niger, River 23
Nigeria 23
Nile, River 9, **20**, **21**, 23
North America 8, **36–39**, 39, 45
North Pole **45**, 45
North Sea 11, 12, 13, 15, **16**, **17**, 17
Northern Ireland **10–12**, 11, 12
Norway **16**, 17

Oceania **32–35**
oceans 8–9
   see also Arctic Ocean, Atlantic Ocean, Indian Ocean, Pacific Ocean
Ottawa 39

Pacific Ocean 8–9, 27, 31, **32**, **33**, 35, 39, 43

Pakistan 29
Panama Canal 39
Papua New Guinea 35
Paris **4**, 9, 19, **40**
Perth 35
Peru **41**, 43
Poland 17
Portugal 15, 19
Pyrenees, mountains **18**, 19

rainforest **21**, **33**, **41**, **42**, **43**
Rhine, River 15, **16**, 17
Rio de Janerio **42**, 43
Rocky Mountains 8, **36**, 39
Romania **19**, 19
Rome **18**, 19
Russia 9, 15, **18**, **26–27**, 26–27

Sahara Desert 9, **20**, 23
Saint Petersburg **26**, 26
Sao Paulo **42**, 43
Saudi Arabia **25**, 29
scale, map **6–7**
Scotland **10–12**, 11, 12
Siberia **26**, 27
Spain 15, 19
South Africa **22**, 23
South America 8, **40–43**, 43, 44
South Pole **44**, 44
Stockholm **17**
Sudan **23**, 23
Suez Canal 23
Sweden 15, 17
Switzerland **14**, 17
Sydney 9, **34**, 35

Tanzania **21**, 23
Tokyo **30**, 31
Turkey 29

Ukraine 17, **18**
United Kingdom **10–13**, 11, 12, 13, 15, 17
United States of America 8, **36–39**, 39
Ural Mountains 26–27

Vatican City **18**
Venezuela **40**, 43
Victoria, Lake 23
Vladivostok 27
volcano **21**, **32**
Volga, River 26

Wales **10**, **11**, 13
Washington D.C. 39
Wellington 35

Zaire, River **21**, 23

Animals of the World

Animals with a * by their name are endangered or may soon be endangered. That means they are in danger of becoming extinct.

Europe   fox   red deer   red squirrel   otter*   rabbit   stork

badger   puffin   pipistrelle bat   hedgehog   grey wolf

Africa   lion   giraffe   crocodile*   wildebeest   ostrich   gazelle*

African elephant*   hippopotamus   zebra*   gorilla*   black rhinoceros*

Asia   Indian elephant*   yak (wild yak*)   snow leopard*   black bear*

giant panda*   tiger*   oryx*   Bactrian camel*   king cobra   orang-utan   Komodo dragon*

Oceania   wombat*   possum*   kookaburra   echidna*   kiwi

koala   bird of paradise   kangaroo   tuatara*   emu   giant tortoise*

North America   porcupine   bald eagle   bison

beaver   grizzly bear   moose   puma*   rattlesnake   raccoon   alligator

South America   jaguar*   golden lion tamarin*   emerald tree boa   macaw   Llama   sloth*

peccary   giant anteater*   armadillo   ocelot*   howler monkey

Antarctica   blue whale*

elephant seal   penguin

Arctic   caribou   snowy owl   musk ox

polar bear*   Arctic fox